PUT YOUR DAMN PHONE DOWN

Glenn Manton

Glenn Manton is a former professional athlete turned author, media personality, youth advocate and professional speaker. He played over 200 games of AFL football for powerhouse teams Essendon and Carlton and was a member of the 1995 Carlton Premiership side. In 1999 he co-founded Whitelion, a not-for-profit organisation assisting youth in crisis within the juvenile justice system and beyond. Glenn's media credits include stints on *The Footy Show*, Vega 91.5, 3RRR and various Foxtel programs, his own shows at the Melbourne Comedy Festival and Fringe Festival, as well as regular columns for *The Age* and *MX* newspapers. He is the author of an autobiography, *Dead Bolt*; and a football dictionary, *Mongrel Punts and Hard Ball Gets*. He lives in Melbourne.

PUT YOUR DAMN PHONE DOWN

Sometimes you've got
to disconnect to reconnect ...

GLENN MANTON

XOUM

First published in Xoum by Brio Books in 2018

Brio Books Pty Ltd
PO Box Q324, QVB Post Office,
NSW 1230, Australia
www.briobooks.com.au

ISBN 978-1-925589-64-1 (print)
ISBN 978-1-925589-65-8 (digital)

Cataloguing-in-publication data is available from the National Library of Australia

Cover design by Xou Creative
Printed in China through Asia Pacific Offset Limited

Papers used by Brio Books are natural, recyclable products made from wood grown
in sustainable forests. The manufacturing processes conform to the environmental
regulations of the country of origin.

I'd like to dedicate this book to – 1990

How to use this book

I'm not about to preach to you. What's the point?
My opinions are mine, the result of my experience.

And yours are yours.

Believe what you will.

Live exactly as you choose.

Your life is yours. Yours alone.

And my life is mine.

Each of my extraordinary triumphs.

And each of my spectacular stuff-ups.

My responsibility alone.

However I would like to share with you one thought-slash-philosophy-slash-principal that I live by which I believe is relevant to your use of this book.

Here goes.

Even though I'd like to believe in reincarnation, I don't.

I don't believe I get a second chance at this life. There are no do-overs.

I believe in the here and the now. And I believe in the future.

If I'm not giving everything to this life, believing I get a second chance at its conclusion, then what am I doing? For all I know, I may be reincarnated as a one-legged seagull desperately chasing a hot chip by the beach. Now, I love the idea of being able to fly and I love the sun and sand, but is that the life I want to live?

Hell no!

So I've made my choice.

Live now.

Give absolutely everything you have despite the risks. Despite the pain. Despite the fact that sometimes life is not fair or just or right. I'm not focused on perfection or being 'the best' – these are false pursuits.

My focus is placed squarely on my integrity and authenticity. I live my life.

And you should live yours.

I say this because how you choose to use this book is up to you. It's your life. Your book. The effort you put in. The research. The thinking. The people you share it with. The conversations. That's all up to you. Your integrity and authenticity will be reflected in your actions and your result. It's really pretty simple.

Inside you'll find stories and recollections alongside questions for you to consider. There are no right or wrongs. Accompanying most of the questions is a reference that I've found relevant, powerful and memorable. Each represents an opportunity for you to dig deeper. There are drawings, movies, songs, articles, photographs and even podcasts. Share them with family and friends. Look at them together. Discuss and debate them.

You'll probably need your phone to do so. And some data. Because your phone isn't all bad. Used thoughtfully your phone is one hell of a tool. Your phone can connect you to information, ideas and conversation. It just has a habit of distracting you (and me) from the here and now.

As a result we miss moments with family, friends and the world around us that will never come again.

It's just a matter of you choosing to use it to isolate or connect.

Prologue

Once I realised they were gone, so was I.

_____

They didn't notice. Not one of them. I slipped away past the incoherent conversation, scrap-laden dinner plates and all the empty bottles. White. Red. White. Red. Red. Oh, and the collection of short and long necks sitting proudly beside them. All were empty bar the dregs.

I'd never thought much of the environment or the location. It was simply my aunt and uncle's curious home. Architect-designed and ahead of its time, it featured raw, exposed cinder blocks and brightly coloured, sharp-angled internal walls. Part home, part warehouse, part art installation. It oozed inner-city feels. Grimy. Gritty. Replete with nearby housing commission flats that would cast a shadow across a suburb inhabited by starving artists, committed drug users and those looking for bang-for-their buck ahead of the gentrification curve.

I didn't know where that equation left my aunt and uncle, as I was just twelve. I wasn't savvy enough to appreciate all the dots, let alone join them. I was just there with my family for a meal.

I did know, however, that my aunt and uncle were *intellectuals*. Deep thinkers who travelled broadly, indulging a passion for cultures and customs. And I knew you couldn't live where – or as – they did without being affected by the constant barrage of alternative movement, thinking and colour.

The bottles continued to add up as the night wore on. I quietly ascended the wooden stairs to the second floor, looking over my shoulder with every step to see if anyone cared that I wasn't sitting dutifully at the table.

They didn't.

Clusters of framed hallway portraits before foreign landmarks, broken up by brightly painted art and wall-mounted sculptures didn't hold my attention. I'd seen similar before.

Bored, I searched about for ... for what I didn't know. Soon I came across an open door. The library. Instantly I knew I'd found something. I had no idea that something would shape my thinking forever.

Books from floor to the ceiling.

In piles next to chairs.

The odd individual lying about the floor, having rejected the masses.

I looked around the room, questioning my place. Should I be among such company? If so, where to start? I was intimidated by the prospect of discovery and the potential for punishment.

My eyes darted between the door and the opportunity. An opportunity I sensed was beyond my years. I decided to close the door and accept the consequences. If I was to be found leering into pages of promiscuity, I'd get punished. The risk assessed, I pushed forward. I tried to create a sense of stealth by shedding my shoes. I rolled up the sleeves of my grey, marle windcheater and began consuming all the room had on offer.

Book after book. Page after page. Raw words. Explicit illustrations. Bold diagrams. Black and white and full-colour pictures.

I gorged on every morsel of information. The stimulation was intense. No matter what I consumed my mind spun at high rpm banging furiously on its rev limiter, near blown. Or possibly just opened. Opened to possibilities and the absolute fact that where I had imagined the game (of life) to end, other people saw as just the beginning. In every imaginable genre. Without exception.

It was all there before me. Laid out. On paper. Sex. Travel. Music. Fashion. Drugs. Religion. Food. Fantasy. Politics. Counter culture. You name it.

It stuck. All of it. Every word. Every image. Stuck in my twelve-year-old mind.

There have been times since that I've wanted for its removal. But, for the most part, I'm grateful. It caused me to think broadly, seek conversation and, ultimately, work towards understanding (not judging) the world around me and those who inhabit it.

I began developing an appreciation of self. Just who was I?

I decided that knowledge was king. That conversation was an important tool both internally and externally. And that placing a finishing line against my personal development was a mistake.

I left the library exactly as I'd found it and made my way back to the noisy dinner table. Like the adults my head spun. Amid the din I made a promise to always ask questions. To think, appreciate and grow.

I've kept that promise.

Maybe this book will encourage you to do the same.

Intro

Hear your voice above a world of noise.

Share it with those around you. And hear their voices.

Speak freely.

Question. Debate. Appreciate. Grow.

Access information.

Learn from the past.

Create your future. Respect communication.

Value relationships.

Your phone isn't all evil. It connects you with family and friends. It captures moments. Shares music. It can soothe, motivate and educate.

Unfortunately, it can also isolate, irritate and dehumanise. The key to using your phone might be as simple as balance and timing. How much and when?

This book is about building connections within yourself and with those around you.

Think.

Appreciate.

Grow.

Become resilient in both thought and action.

Hear your own voice above a world of noise.

And occasionally ...

PUT YOUR DAMN PHONE DOWN!

Glenn Manton

Darkness

Everyone – regardless of race, religion, culture or socio-economic status – experiences darkness. Weight. Stress. Anxiety. A bad day. Depression. Whatever you want to call it. No amount of good fortune, cotton wool, hard liquor, prescription or illicit drugs can prevent this.

Shit happens. And the light can dim quickly.

Unique to each individual, the feeling is bespoke. One day. Maybe two. A week. Months. Years. A lifetime.

Mental health owns a scale with people at either end and countless in between.

My scales have almost tipped. Life has been heavy, far from a feather. I've felt darkness. Broken. But I don't break. Won't break. I refuse to. Working through the tears I have developed tools. Tools that work for me. Tools that allow me to contain my feelings, process them and move forward.

I talk, *really* talk. To people whom I love and trust. People who love me. I share my struggles. And I use the conversation to grow. I also talk to myself – a lot. Practising of 'self-talk' is central to my wellbeing.

I listen to the global common denominator – music – with abandon. I have playlists for all occasions. I have songs to sing to, cry with, shout at and relax. I have songs that release me, songs that realise me.

Scribbling ideas down and brain-dumping thoughts makes a difference too. I'm forever writing down ideas and purging thoughts onto paper.

I run, box, jump, lift and stretch my way through dark moments. I feel untouchable in the gym. It has become my sanctuary. Fiddling with wrenches and turning screws also helps clear my mind.

Life isn't easy or fair or right or simple. On occasion it seems like all the wrongs pile up about your feet. And with every step they're dragged about with you slowing your progress. Holding you back.

I know that feeling. I also know it's not something I'll ever settle for.

Have you ever been racist?

Watch:
Do the Right Thing

Spike Lee film

A beautifully executed vision.
Forever relevant and powerful.
Mandatory viewing for all.

What is the truth about global warming?

Start researching here: 'Trump v Gore'

Videos, articles, more!

One of many starting points to allow you to cut through to the truth of this divisive topic.

Does everyone have depression?

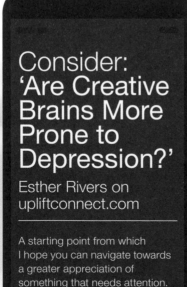

Consider:
'Are Creative Brains More Prone to Depression?'

Esther Rivers on
upliftconnect.com

A starting point from which I hope you can navigate towards a greater appreciation of something that needs attention.

What does it mean to think?

Read:
Illusions

Richard Bach

An afternoon read which caused me to think about 'influence' and further investigate this prominent writer.

Life and death

Live well. Risk. Fall. Hurt. And rise. Go beyond. Three steps beyond what you thought was possible and then another inch. Feel. Feel everything. Share passion. Spread laughter. Fail. Fail many many times. And grow from each experience. Develop integrity. Love. Reject apathy. Ask questions. Think. Exhaust your ideas. Invest your time. Leave space for dreams. And for fantasy. Live your life. Spend your body. Free your mind. Empty your heart. Die well.

Is a 'lifelong' marriage possible?

**Watch:
'The
Invitations'**

Seinfeld

An opportunity to laugh
before considering the
global divorce rate. There
may not be any more
important a topic.

Regrets

I know people who boast of no regrets. Some will offer such comment as a toast in an effort to capture the conversation late into the night – To 'no regrets' – salute!

Some will share it as a form of punctuation when they can't cope with volatile emotions. Others will choose a font and ask a tattooist to pour on the electricity and fire up their gun to ink the words permanently upon their body.

If you have no regrets you're paying life no attention, no respect.

Or you're perfect.

Or an arsehole.

Or worse still, a perfect arsehole.

Here is a short list of 'stuff' I regret in no particular order.

- Allowing Sean Enfield to take the blame and corporal punishment for my actions in primary school.

- Running away from opportunity. Many opportunities. Lots of running. Tired feet.

- Cutting my arm in half as a teenager.

- Telling my dad not to kiss me goodnight.

- Not wanting to control my anger.

- Not wanting to learn how to control my anger.

- Getting my teenage girlfriend pregnant.

- Cheating in maths class. Maths homework. Maths exams. Lots of cheating.

- All the hickeys I placed on Kirsten Davidson's neck at lunchtime in high school.

- Anytime I wasn't myself.

- Using my phone while driving.

- Thinking that 'she' defined my value.

- Thinking that 'they' were more valuable than me.

- Shadow boxing with fear.

- Trying cigarettes.

- Boat shoes.

- Giving a ***k about nothing.

- Not knowing the subtle art of not giving a ***k.

- Missing Nirvana in concert.

- Missing INXS in concert.

- Missing Nas in concert.

- Holding onto toxic relationships.

- Entertaining toxic people.

- Not handing in the wallet full of money I found next to a table-top Galaga machine one summer.

- Every text message sent after 3 am.

- Getting my hair permed.

- Punching a wall.

- Allowing Mary Ellis to upset me.

- Breaking the limbo pole because I was too tall to limbo under it.

- Eating a family-sized El-Nacho pizza alone in my car and the effects thereafter.

- Any time I chose to communicate poorly.

- Joining Facebook.

What is celebrity?

Read:
The Celebrity
Death List
Website

A fascinating example of
our collective obsession to
promote people by labelling
them 'celebrity'.

What is history's most important lesson?

Watch: Metallica's 'One'

I clearly remember watching this clip late into the night and being chilled by its concept and haunted by the intense drumming.

How do people become homeless?

Read:
Iskhandar
Razak's ABC
article about
Japan's
invisible
homeless

A social issue that doesn't
discriminate. Life's a game of
snakes and ladders. Ignoring
the 'snakes' sees you bitten.

Is
fantasy
better
than
reality?

Listen:
'Are video games a waste of time?'

BBC podcasts

Just one of the many perspectives at play here. How many can you appreciate?

Adam's song

Everything has a backstory, a reason, a series of bread crumbs that lead home. You're either familiar with the narrative or you're guessing, having stumbled across a crumb or two.

The 90s pop-punk band Blink-182 didn't always have a bunch of random numbers behind their original name, Blink – they used a hyphen to hitch 182 to their wagon when legal action was threatened by an Irish band with the same name. I thought that the 182 was a reference to *Star Wars*, in particular, the number of times Luke Skywalker blinked in the original movie. I remember trying to count for myself but pretty soon lost interest. I'd also heard that 182 was a reference to the number of expletives Al Pacino uttered in *Scar Face*. Either way, I have no idea why the trio of Californian-based musicians chose that number. You'd have to ask them. Nor am I sure why someone would choose to take their own life. You'd have to ask them that, too.

Blink-182 churned out quite a few hits that helped define a generation finding its feet atop skateboards while questioning the need to conform. Generation Y was in full swing when they released 'Adam's Song' in September 2000. It was quickly labelled a 'suicide song'. I remember being struck by the stylistic change for a band that was known for being immature. I loved songs like 'Josie' and 'Dammit' from their second album *Dude Ranch*. They featured classic coming-of-age themes with hard driving guitars, crashing drums and kitsch film clips. Given the title of their third album *Enema of the State*, I thought the bread crumbs would lead to more of the same.

I was wrong. 'Adam's Song' was different, the type of tune that has you questioning whether to sing along or stay silent. It promoted debate. And that's a good thing.

I'd felt like I'd never conquered.

I'd felt like an unknown.

I'd felt like the best days were behind me.

There were layers to 'Adam's Song' much like the act itself and its associates: isolation, depression and of course backstory. The first verse ends with the line 'You'll be sorry when I'm gone'. Those words always struck me as being rhetorical.

Old cartoons often had characters dying due to ill-fated acts with their ghostly silhouettes floating towards heaven, the character often chastising themselves as they went. I picture someone who has chosen to take their own life as having a similar conversation. I imagine they question such a permanent action and that they feel sorrow for both themselves and those around them. Suicide seems like a mistake, which many people tragically make, and many more have to live with. But I don't know. I'm just guessing.

I've contemplated it without much conviction. My backstory never seemed to justify it. Not that I know the equation. Assuming your mental health mirrors someone else's is shallow. 'Adam's Song' definitely added to my thinking, to my compassion. Its narrative plays out each and every day under a different name. For many, I'm sure a cry for help is answered by the silence of death. I don't need to collect bread crumbs to appreciate that. But I'm also sure that the song helps people explore their backstories and better understand their own situations. And with a bit of luck create different futures.

At times I still feel like I've never conquered. I still feel like an unknown and that my best days are behind me. But I choose to believe that 'tomorrow holds such better days'. And that I can live them.

Watch: Eddie Izzard's 'Death Star Canteen'

Skit

A confronting comedian whose 'position' on sexuality may assist you in finding yours.

Do people choose their sexuality?

Do we choose how we die?

Watch:
CNN story about Sarajevo's 'Romeo and Juliet'

A multi-layered piece I found to be in equal parts uplifting and devastating.

Is it okay to experiment with drugs?

Watch:
The Basketball Diaries

Scott Kalvert film

The classic cautionary tale of losing oneself to a misplaced direction.

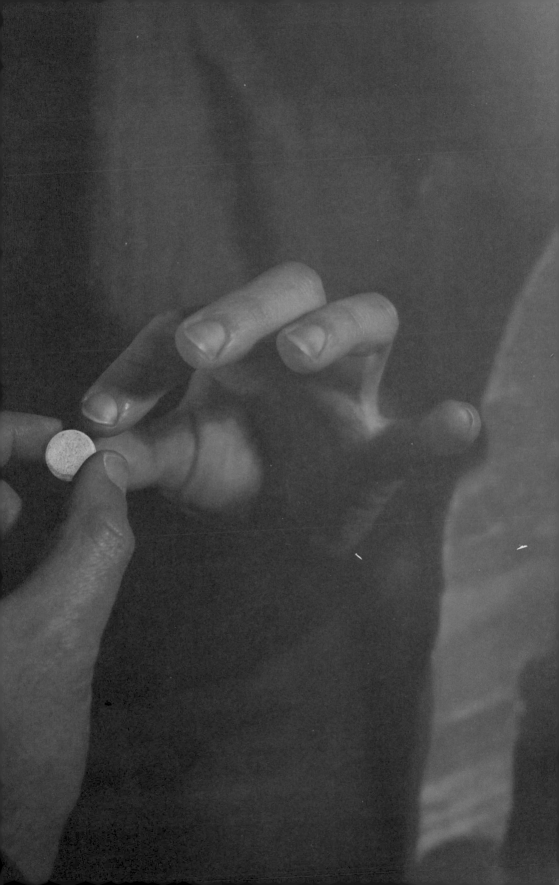

Muffins

I'd go out of my way to get my dirty paws on a muffin. Or three. Fresh baked daily with organic ingredients just as you'd expect from a health conscious café. If you were lucky they'd be over-cooked, giving each one a crisp, crunchy exterior that married perfectly with the soft apple, banana, dates or chocolate chunks inside. Yeah, you could say I have a sweet tooth.

Sadly that café is now closed. It was gutted, made over and replaced by a hipster butchers where the staff wear black Bowler hats and striped aprons. It's a bit much to be honest but I guess it plays to a market that's prepared to pay top dollar for exclusive cuts of meat. But what would I know. I'm a vegetarian.

The muffins were always reasonably priced. You could get three for fifteen bucks and pocket some change. And if you timed it just right one of the bohemian staff might throw in a extra muffin before tying her dreads up and hooking into the post-lunch clean-up. I had meetings at that café. Inner-city catch-ups, business or otherwise. It was central and local. Nobody ever objected.

I remember meeting a guy there one autumn afternoon. We exchanged pleasantries and sat halfway down the elongated seating area which butted up to the galley style kitchen. From where I sat I could see the muffins on the counter top. I could barely contain my enthusiasm. And yet at some point during the smalltalk I asked the guy if we could leave. Just up and go – move across the rumbling inner city street to the patisserie opposite. I have no idea why. It certainly wasn't so I could use the four years of French I studied and failed in high school.

The guy obliged and we 'Froggered' our way across the road, through the door and into the patisserie. I can recall how the door opened to the right, where the counter was, the display cabinets, the bain-marie, the buzzing fridge and the off-white chairs and tables which were populated by elderly customers. Funny thing is I can't remember the name of the guy. Or why we were meeting.

As we settled into our new surrounds I noticed something outside. I abruptly excused myself and lunged for the door before shouting a girl's name down the street.

A gaunt, dishevelled man wearing oversized clothing standing on the corner stopped when he heard my call. He looked back at me. He knew who I was and I knew him. And I hated him. My parents had taught me not to hate but that didn't matter.

We stared at each other before he said something. Seconds later a small blonde girl rounded onto the main road, took one look at me and ran straight into my arms. I hugged her. As we embraced 'he' joined us. I shocked myself when I gently lowered her to the ground and extended my hand to shake his.

'Have you eaten?' I asked them. They hadn't.

Moments later we were back in the patisserie. The other patrons looked uneasy which wasn't lost on the staff. The guy I was meeting excused himself and left without so much as a word. I imagined the sight and smell of two hardened drug addicts was a little full-on.

We sat front and centre and allowed the crowd to gawk as I ordered three orange juices and a couple of croissants. I wasn't hungry. We spoke about old times and those upcoming; what had changed and what had stayed the same. Sadly, the answers were all too familiar. Beneath the girl's heavy foundation her skin seemed to crawl. Her eyes pretended to be full. I couldn't look at his.

I'd met her in jail. She was an inmate, I was a guest, the type invited to inspire. We connected and began talking; the main subject matter – writing. She loved to scribble and scrawl and her thinking was deep, lateral and confronting. After years of physical, psychological and emotional abuse, she filled countless diaries with her raw, untempered thoughts. Day after week after month on the streets. Times remembered in pen and pencil. Sometimes in colour and always hard to read. Her writing was better than mine.

Over the next four years I visited her regularly. In and thankfully back out of jail on the same day. A little time here, a little more there. I watched her get better, almost well again. From day one I'd seen something small in her writing that I wanted to support. She became a little sister to me. I cared about her, and wanted to see her exchange a needle for a pen on a permanent basis.

My optimism was misguided. She plunged a needle back into her arm the day she was released. 'He' had been released the exact same day. Who cross-checks this shit?

It broke my heart.

Back in the patisserie, the pair slurped at their orange juices before excusing themselves.

'Thank you,' she said.

We embraced. Again I shook his hand. And they left. I've not seen either of them since.

She was a fifteen-year-old private school girl who decided to wag one day. Catching a train from the burbs to the city, she met him as she left the station. He offered her the chance to shoot heroin. She said yes.

Is there ever justification for war?

View:
Nick Ut's photo of Phan Thị Kim Phúc aka the 'Napalm Girl'

Photograph

A incredibly powerful image that I'd prefer to ignore but never could.

What does **religion** mean to you?

Read:
VICE News
on religion
Website

A valuable site that provides
an opportunity to investigate
our beliefs.

What is fear?

Watch:
Jane Elliot's
'Brown
Eyes vs
Blue Eyes'
YouTube video

A social experiment
that deeply affected me.

Taste the pain

August the 16th, 1989. The Red Hot Chili Peppers released their fourth studio album *Mother's Milk*. Track four – 'Knock me down' – felt right. It made sense. I'd found something that fit. I was sixteen.

Every time I listened to the song I heard something new. A frantic bass pluck I'd previously missed. Deeper shades of Hendrix in the guitar sound. Passion-filled drumming that offered more than just a time check.

49

And yet it wasn't until after I needed it the most that 'Knock me down' shared a lyric that would ultimately change my life. A lyric that had I been able to appreciate and absorb that winter would have saved me a great deal of pain in spring a year later.

As the radio edit begins to fade out, lead singer Anthony Kiedis repeats: 'It's so lonely when you don't even know yourself – it's so lonely.'

One, two, three times. And the song dissolves.

I must have listened to those lyrics over a hundred times without truly hearing them.

'It's so lonely when you don't even know yourself – it's so lonely.'

I didn't know myself. Hadn't even thought to try. It was all too easy to ignore the daily inner monologues about stress, anxiety, fear and a good dose of self-loathing. I'd outwardly rebut the truth with anger, arrogance and indifference. Projecting a false me. A hollow self. As a result, I was always alone even when surrounded by others. My thoughts belonged to the masses, with my actions one step behind.

As 1989 drew to a close I decided to dedicate my life to the appreciation of self. I wanted to know who I was. How I thought. What I valued.

And how to hold onto these values when tested.

I made that decision while alone in a hospital bed late one Saturday night, my right arm literally having been cut in half at the elbow. I felt little physical pain yet my mind ached. Throbbed. I'd been puffing out my chest in order to hide my disconnect. I was trying too hard. I was a false hero. I owned no cape.

The surgeon's stark words were fresh and final.

'You're a right joke,' he said in his thick English accent. 'You have no idea who you are. You will be the last person I perform surgery on tonight. I suggest you lie upon that hospital bed and have a good think about who you are.'

As the nurse drew the curtain, the doctor gestured for her to stop. He looked at her with purpose and then pointed toward the doorknob in his hand.

'Do you see this?' he asked me.

I nodded solemnly.

'You will never turn one of these again. But that isn't your problem. Your problem is you don't know who you are.'

With that he motioned for the nurse to finish drawing the curtain and together they left the room.

Among all the tears, the anger and the regret that followed, I found the smallest piece of courage. Courage I have accessed every day since that night to look at myself and ensure I saw reality.

Who was your first crush?

Read:
An article about Serina (*Battlestar Galactica*)

Wikipedia entry

I've always thought Jane Seymour attractive. However I had no idea she played the TV character in whom I became 'crushed-up' until I researched this question.

Listen to:
'Castles
Made of
Sand'

Jimi Hendrix

The various characters
within this song and
their stories have always
caused me to reflect.

Name a song that has impacted your life?

Glenn Manton

The drive

Give me a good stretch of road. Nothing dead straight. Switchbacks. Long sweepers. Something that sees you cut through the landscape or find balance against the coast. The kind that really involves the driver; that pins a smile to your face and clears your head. Every cobweb. Every stress. Gone. Lost in the exhaust note of a well-sorted '73 BMW 2002 with huffing twin Webbers. Or the distinctive 'boxer' rumble of an early Porsche 911.

Some say it's sacrilegious to entertain the idea of listening to anything other than an engine's peaks and troughs. It's hard to disagree. The sound of deep induction and over-run crackles are intoxicating. But so is music.

I combine both. The best of both worlds. I cannot build a vehicle from scratch like Mr Rapp or Ferdinand Porsche. I'm just not that good on the tools. But I can create a playlist to complement their vision, the landscape and her.

There's a time for solitude. A space to sit in isolation. But it's better when she is there. By my side listening together. Sharing our feels, music the common denominator.

Track one
Vallis Alps – *Young*

Track two
Flight Facilities – *Stranded*

Track three
Raving George – *Oscar and the wolf*

Track four
Rufus – *Take me*

Are your real-world and offline personalities the same?

Watch:
MTV's
Catfish TV

An 'interesting' piece that demonstrates the complex web that is human behaviour.

Consider this

Put your damn phone down.

For a moment or two at least. And speak about Indian food and its consequences, chewing tobacco during baseball games, why men grow hipster beards but don't pluck their ear hair, bad sunburn marks, the value of spot tests, ripe bananas, marijuana, sea monkeys, bears and honey, urban greeting techniques, backyard bbq's for vegans, how to effectively pack a suitcase, colloquial slang, a cow's responsibility, the misguided tongues of cheap shoes, the theory of anything, bats, love, pirañas, bats that love pirañas, annoying sounds, hates, likes, lust, life, peace, sexual tension, rock and roll, the diminishing Amazon jungle, living on a prayer, what real happiness costs, Vegemite, forever, punk attitude and the cost of hairspray, space, outer space, MySpace, varieties of cakes and donuts, lobsters and why they are misunderstood, *JAWS*, the truth, mountains to climb or just photograph, the beauty of risk, magic tricks, grass stain removal and where goldfish actually go when flushed down the toilet.

What are your thoughts on refugees?

Read:
VICE News
on refugees

A starting point from which to thoughtfully explore a topic that regularly divides.

Does every life have the same value?

View:
The 'vulture and the little girl'

Kevin Carter photograph

An opportunity to look beyond your environment and level of privilege.

Loss

Wogs poured concrete. That's what I thought. Old-school wogs. Overly hairy men with handkerchiefs tied about their heads. The type who could visually balance his stomach bulge and arse crack. An art in itself, though the result was never anything to look at. I imagined that was the type of man who'd poured the mix upon which I uncomfortably sat. Thin concrete curbing; my impromptu seat. My head bowed, my hands obscuring my face, tears tracked down my cheeks and fell with purpose; the bluestones glistening with every addition.

I had no interest in lifting my head. I didn't want to engage – with anyone. Had the earth beneath me split in two I would have allowed it to swallow me whole, falling to the earth's core, hell – or whatever came first. Such relief would have been welcome.

Despite my want there would be no tectonic movement. Everything stayed just as it was. My head remained down. The tears kept falling. The concrete curbing continued to add to my discomfort.

I imagined the world around me slowing to look at the train wreck on the curbing. Gawking. It didn't matter whether I looked up or not for in my mind I was surrounded by people – all of whom were judging me. Staring. Pointing. Each of them shaking their heads. Their imagined comments polluting mine.

It felt like I sat there forever. The nurse told me to go outside and wait about twenty minutes. I tried counting the time out in my head. Twelve hundred seconds. I thought I could distract myself, focus on something else. One cat and dog. Two cat and dog. Three cat and dog. I couldn't concentrate and didn't make it past twenty-seven. Without a watch, I'd just have to guess when to return.

Not that I wanted to go back inside. It made me uncomfortable. It was clean. Modern. A clinic. Staffed by professionals dressed in crisp white medical garb. And yet I felt so uneasy. It was the guilt, no doubt. And the shame. I'd been told. Clearly.

I thought I heard her scream as I was ushered outside; I wanted to be there to support her; felt like it was all my fault. The door she entered was closed as I looked back over my shoulder. I could only imagine what was going on inside.

I stood briefly on the first floor landing wondering if I should wait by the front door. The clinic was housed in a beautiful terrace with stoop-like stairs, ornate furnishings about the balustrades and lead-light about the door. The garden was well maintained. Despite the visual I didn't want to be associated with the place. I knew the truth.

So I made my way down the stairs, along the path and through the heavy iron gate to the busy road out front. Unexpectedly, a narrow laneway appeared just a few metres from the gate. I took it, turning down its cobbled path, and sat down on the concrete curbing. Alone. Like her.

Teens have abortions. Stupid teens. Overly confident types with deftly styled hair who think with their dicks. The types who can balance indifference with a smile. An art in itself, though the result was nothing to emulate.

I thought that's what the wogs would say as I sat on their concrete next to the clinic waiting for it to all be over. For her to be okay. Not knowing that I'd never be able to shake the regret for the action and all the pain it caused.

What is in our food?

Read:
eatingyou
alive.co

Website

We are what we eat.
And what we eat can
be confronting as many
manufacturers prioritise
shelf space for quality.

Listen:
'How
powerful is
Facebook's
algorithm?'
BBC podcast

An aspect of life that
deserves your full attention.
And considered action.

Can the
media
**be
trusted?**

Does
more
money
equal
**more
problems?**

Watch:
Eric B and
Rakim's
classic clip
for 'Paid
in full'

Familiarise yourself with
rap royalty and the age-old
question.

Watch:
American
snowboarder
Lindsey
Jacobellis at
the 2006 Turin
Olympics

For every action there is a
reaction. Appreciating failure
is a key to achieving success.

What is
failure?

Bonfire

I remember the wail of sirens over lusting engines as drivers tried to navigate a path across the city. Trams would ring their bells as they jostled for position among the early evening traffic. And dogs barking. I clearly remember dogs barking. Most likely at the moon, as dogs do. And yet I felt sure. Safe. I knew exactly where I was. I found the roar of the bonfire reassuring. A constant presence that soothed all those gathered about it. I was no different.

The sun had long since dipped and with it the ability to identify who else was there. Not that it mattered. The bonfire was a meeting point. A place where everyone was equal. The city's issues found a bandaid as the fire crackled and popped. Time stood still. Minutes became hours. Anything flammable was heaped upon the flames. And it burnt brightly, trailing off into the night sky. This was a place to listen, to absorb. No one asked questions. They just seemed to rise like embers and disappear for another time. Bodies would roll out from depressing inner city commission buildings to escape. Others would travel further. Much further. Each just a shape against the night. The occasional mohawk provided some definition. My mind was open. I held no fear. No anxiety. I observed. I listened. I worked out my place among the group. Despite a lack of written rules, everything worked. No one questioned your race or religion. Your sexual preference wasn't an issue. Nor your wealth. You simply stood around the fire and talked. You shared your stories and welcomed others. Stories of sleepless nights with a new love. Of fresh cherry Docs and the hard earned it took to buy them. Of jimmying car badges with screwdrivers.

I remember multiple tape decks spitting diversity. INXS, Public Enemy and the Dead Kennedys head to head at the mercy of double D batteries. Music was the common denominator. Each track a moment that stood alone. Occasionally a rotating flash would burst ahead of a photograph that may or may not have been worth developing the next day at the local chemist. Pot luck at best.

In the early morning it would all end, not that I ever stayed that late. The fire would eventually expire and with it the night itself. I imagined that all those about it would stumble or skip home. To whatever home they had. A piece of cardboard on the doorstep of the town hall. An over-crowded apartment housing generations. A share house crawling with uni students.

Or my home. A picture-book cream brick veneer. Every nuclear family's dream.

I remember lying in bed trying to digest it all. And I remember thinking just how lucky I was. My lot wasn't so bad. I had options. Clear pathways that others would never realise. I always slept well after those bonfire nights.

How does advertising affect you?

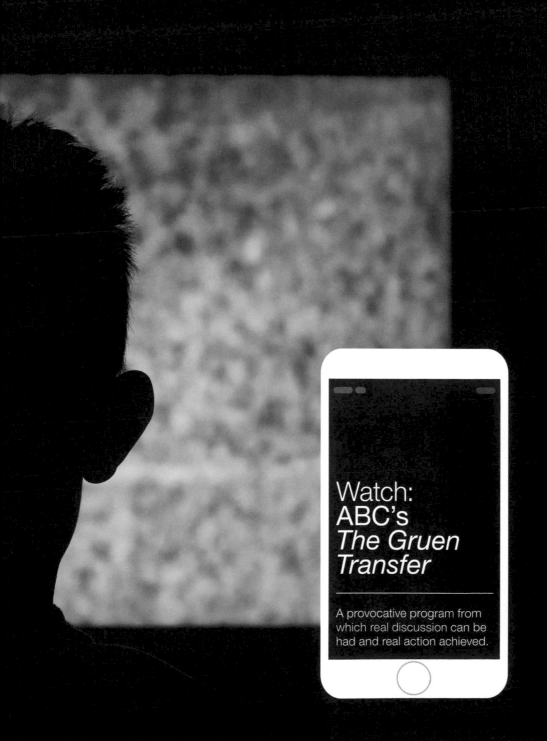

Watch:
ABC's
*The Gruen
Transfer*

A provocative program from
which real discussion can be
had and real action achieved.

What
is art?

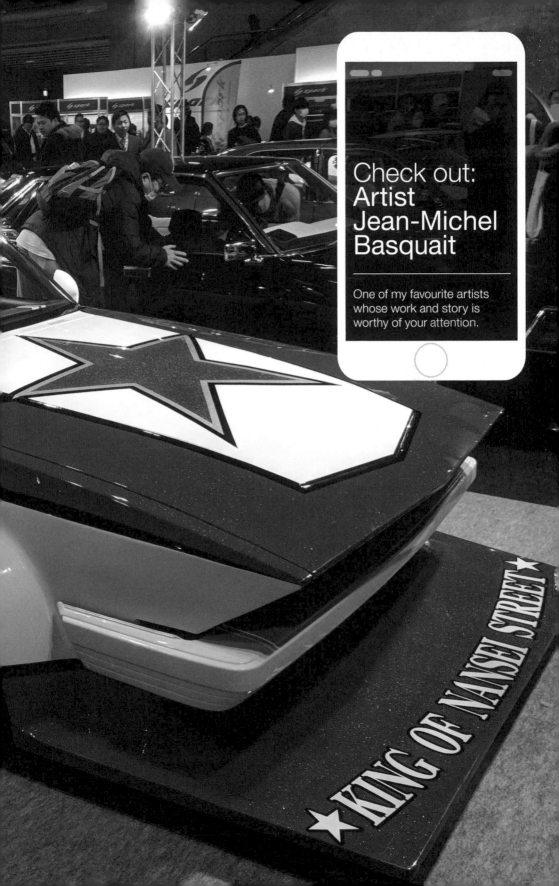

Check out: Artist Jean-Michel Basquait

One of my favourite artists whose work and story is worthy of your attention.

Already gone

Dave Grohl was wrong. Howling 'Everlong' at the moon didn't change a thing. With every breath I'd tried to expel you. Holding you inside made me ill. Warped my perspective. Trapped me.

I'd tried lots of alternatives. Lyrical tweezers. Go-to songs which had helped place emotions in the past. Ben Harper's collaboration with Vanessa Da Mata 'Boa sorte' was a gift that failed. Mazzy Star's 'Fade into you' left me numb regardless of the volume. 'Clarity' by Foxes would wrap my heart around a power pole with every listen.

The closest I came was Alison Wonderland's 'Already gone'. It felt like the lyrics were stolen straight from your playbook. Every damn word rang true and I quickly learnt each of them. The song made sense and became an anthem. It was the right song at the right time. I'd sing it quietly in my head when in public and scream it with venom when I was alone. But it didn't cleanse the bitter aftertaste. Not until I saw it live. Not until Alison unexpectedly dialled it up a notch – or two – and chose to share a dirty trap remix. Epic bass drops and the thick horns that would proceed them dissolved every last memory. Surrounded by a mass of silhouettes your memory seeped into the night sky to be forever forgotten. Finally you were gone. My mind cleansed.

Two turntables, a mixing desk and deft ears equalled freedom.

The crowd helped me to forgive myself. Their energy complemented mine. I climbed inside the barrel of a surging wall of sound and rode it out. The process cleansed me. It took longer than I imagined. Longer than ever before. My inability to correctly process all that had happened meant your memory lingered long after my respect, let alone the love, had died. I was dumb, in fact, just plain stupid. I allowed myself to be manipulated. You asked for time, space and more time. I provided both although you were 'already gone'. Time wasted along with emotions as you repositioned yourself at my expense. An all-too-common game from which you should always walk away. I knew that. But I didn't.

I can't remember what track Alison dialled in next that night but I do remember feeling my heart exhale, my head clear and my body come alive. The night ended with a musical climax of vibrant colour and sound followed by still night air. A moment or two later the crowd gathered their thoughts and came to life. I was ahead of the curve. My thoughts galvanised. A new beginning. A change in direction.

Adjusting the rear-view mirror I chose to never look back again.

Do we choose how we love?

Are we free?

Listen: Klang-karussell's song, 'Netzwerk'

A beautifully crafted song set against a provocative clip that highlights 'choice'.

The Kookaburra

My attitude was masked by the clapping and chanting. Each wave of noise irritated me; the vibrant colour that flooded my perspective was lost upon me. From where I sat everything was grey. I was indifferent to the crowd. Ninety thousand? Ninety-three and a bit. Counting each of them would have been a productive distraction. I was just another number watching, not playing. Insignificant to the on-field narrative. And that was how I felt. Selfishly, that was *all* I could feel.

———————

I'd dreamt of this day. Many have. A day when all eyes look upon you and you bathe in such inspection. A winner. The athlete, the actor, the rockstar or the bride. This day was meant to be yours. Your time to shine.

And yet I couldn't have been more dull; the tarnished athlete sitting uncomfortably in a hard plastic seat digesting some inane half-time entertainment. My mind was fuelled with frustration. Anger. How? Why? One untimely injury and now this. Excused from the big dance. A childhood dream dashed; this type of opportunity didn't happen every year.

Anyway I cut it I missed out. Whichever team won I lost. One team would get to hold the Premiership Cup, each individual wearing their premiership medallion, while the other team got nothing. Despite the fact that my team was competing, I was effectively with the 'other'. Even if my teammates won I didn't. I wanted no part of it. I had no interest. It was theirs not mine. I couldn't justify a smile or a post-game celebration. What was I celebrating?

So I sat in a cocoon of petulance hoping the game's second half would somehow accelerate and the misery would be over along with what remained of a wasted year. 1993.

Suddenly a large thick hand fell upon my shoulder. Startled, I looked up to see a foreign face. Before I could say a word the stranger spoke.

'You're a very good footballer.'

My chest swelled and the storm cloud about me began to rise. I was going to reply but he cut me off.

'But you're not that good.'

The cloud returned. And the anger rose. Who was this guy? Before I could return fire he pulled out a pen and a scrap of paper. He wrote his name and number on it then folded it carefully in half.

'Call me if you'd like to become a better footballer and a better person.'

Shocked, I took the piece of paper and jammed it into the inside pocket of my blazer. When I looked up, he was gone.

I spent the second half oscillating between the game and that piece of paper. The bloke's name was Alec. Alec Epis. And he called himself 'The Kookaburra'.

I wanted to throw the piece of paper on the ground to join the rest of the rubbish. But instead I kept it. I figured it could rot away quietly, forgotten along with the day.

The game was soon over. My team won. My teammates wore their medals proudly, boisterous in victory. Everyone held the Premiership Cup. Everyone except me.

As soon as I got home my father started asking questions I didn't want to answer. It didn't take long for me to rudely suggest that all I had to show for the day was a scrap of paper from some bloke who called himself 'The Kookaburra'.

My father fell silent. 'You met "The Kookaburra"?'

'You know him?'

'Yes.'

'Well, who is he?'

Highly animated, my father quickly told me all about the former footy legend. Then he asked me, 'What did he say to you?'

'He told me to call him if I wanted to be a better footballer. And a better person. What do I do?'

'Call him!' said my father. 'Call him now.'

I turned to my mother who was quietly preparing dinner. 'Should I?'

'Only if he has patience,' she said without losing focus.

The decision made, I picked up the receiver and dialled the Kookaburra's number. The process seemed to take forever as the mechanism spun backwards allowing the next number to be entered.

His phone began to ring. Nervously I waited for my call to be answered.

'Alec speaking.'

I froze for a moment before saying my name and the reason for my call.

Within seconds I lost control of the conversation. I was told to meet on Wednesday at 7 am at a local park. Clarinda Reserve at the bottom of Park Street. I knew it. I'd driven past it many times. It wasn't far from home.

I agreed.

'Great. I'll see you there at 7 am.' *Click*.

With the phone still at my ear I stood wondering what I had just done.

Wednesday seemed to take forever to arrive. With the thrill of playing each week gone, the off season was boring. Dragging myself out of bed at 7 am I arrived at Clarinda Reserve at 7.15 am and swaggered my way towards a barrel-chested Italian who leant upon a wheelie bin smack damn in the middle of the park.

By the time I reached him it was 7.17 am.

He looked angry. At me? It was too late to turn back. My feet were set.

He exploded. A combination of physical threats, saliva and every known expletive wrapped succinctly in a venomous tirade. I was told that should I ever choose to be late again never to come back. I thought that suggestion just fine as I had clearly engaged a psychopath. A nutter. Someone who was well beyond the spectrum. The whole 'Kookaburra' thing was a dead giveaway. How did I miss it?

For now though I was trapped. The equation was simple. Gut out this session. Return to my car. Drive home to the sanctuary of parents I already knew I couldn't relate to and never spend another second with the Kookaburra.

I didn't think things could get any worse. But they did. For two hours he verbally abused me and physically tested me, putting me through drill after drill with no respite. In the end I was completely spent. The needle was on empty as I dragged myself back to my car. Slumping behind the steering wheel I promised never to spend another second with Alec Epis. Driving home I chanted the promise to myself. Over and over. Not another second. Not one.

My lower back tight, my hamstrings screaming, I was sore for days afterwards.

Religiously I kept that chant going.

But then something changed.

Just like that.

I decided to go back. On Wednesday. Back to Clarinda Reserve at the bottom of Park Street. At 7 am.

I called Alec to confirm my attendance. This time I wasn't late.

He flogged me again. Abusing me every step of the way.

I promised never to go back.

Again I changed my mind. And again he flogged me.

Alec and I met at 7 am each Wednesday morning at Clarinda Reserve at the bottom of Park Street for the next nine years. We never missed a Wednesday. Not one.

I became a better footballer and a better person. His promise true.

———————————————————

In 1995 I grasped the Premiership Cup while wearing a bright silver medallion around my neck. In a moment of silence away from the bullshit and bluster winners feel, I realised that the scrap of paper I'd received on the same date two years earlier was a far more valuable acquisition.

What would you do if you had 24 hours to live?

OPEN
4HRS

Watch:
*Organic
apple pie*
on Culinary
Butterfly

Website

I believe the best
conversations occur in
the kitchen with those
we love.

AURANT

Addiction

A cloud hangs low about you.

You always felt the weight of your past. Down to the gram.

Set fast baggage you never fought to shake. You lacked perspective. It was never just you.

Your story was not unique. Just unique to you.

It was always easier to place the blame and kit up.

What a job lot.

There was no doubting your beauty. Your potential was never questioned.

From the full-colour description that was shared I can picture your numb face as your skin was punctured and your 'escape' injected.

I can imagine you slumped in the shop doorway.

Closed for business.

Your bare legs protruding onto the sidewalk like hurdles.

People stepped right over, so I was told.

The world doesn't stop. Never will.

That needle could never pin-point your dreams.

Your pursed lips tasted the gritty concrete as your eyes emptied of life. One armed pinned beneath your torso.

Did you hear the wail of sirens?

The sound of strangers rushing to save you from your inner hatred.

God knows I'd tried. Over and over again.

And now this?

All fears realised as the slate grey blanket was placed over your body.

I'm told it matched your face.

A final withdrawal from us all.

You maxed your card.

It's processed. Only paperwork remains.

How does criticism affect you?

Check out:
The mysterious
British artist
Banksy

Equal parts applauded
and condemned. A dedicated
artist may be the epitome
of resilience.

What does it mean to think?

Sanctuary

Sometimes, late at night, I sit on a park bench by the water, bumping tunes and looking over at the city glowing on the other side. I love soaking this up – my ears are full of music and the city looks full of possibilities.

Every now and then, an overflowing container ship blocks the view. I slip off my headphones and hear the sound of the ship cutting through the water and tug boats blasting their horns. I don't know where they've come from, but the port isn't far now.

I want to feel that kind of relief. I want to feel like the port isn't far. I want that mental sanctuary. That's why I come here.

I want to dive into life and its questions and all the potential answers, even though they are so vast. But I'm okay with that. We're never all going to think the same way.

I want to be thoughtful, smart – able to stand with conviction. Able to stand against the tide if necessary. I'm not trying to be right. I'm just trying to be right for me.

The air is still and I gaze at that city and I think, each thought my own.

What's your favourite photo?

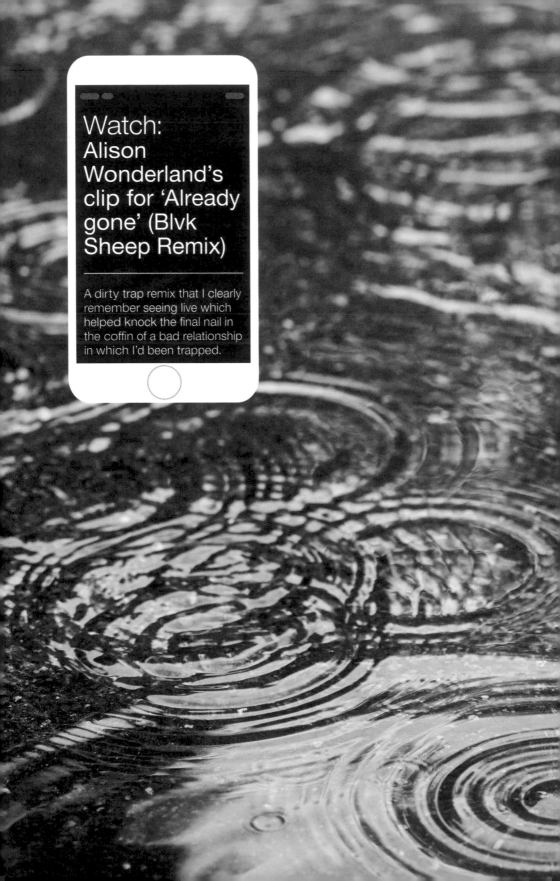

Watch:
Alison
Wonderland's
clip for 'Already
gone' (Blvk
Sheep Remix)

A dirty trap remix that I clearly
remember seeing live which
helped knock the final nail in
the coffin of a bad relationship
in which I'd been trapped.

Watch:
The Mighty
Boosh's
'Introducing
Ruby'

YouTube video

Wholistic health is becoming
the benchmark for personal
wellbeing. This clip highlights
the need for a well-rounded
approach.

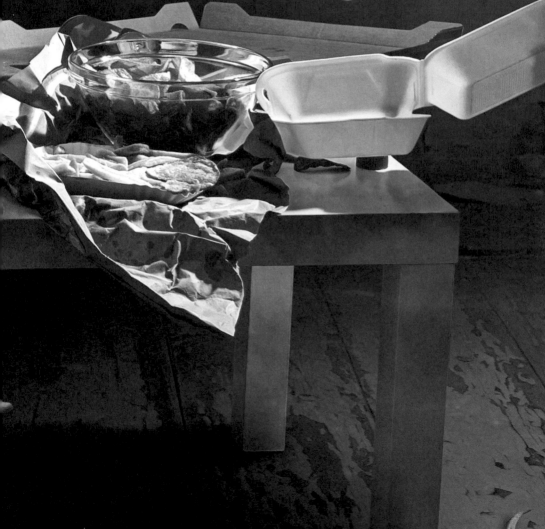

Are you
healthy?

Is
there
life
**beyond
Earth?**

Listen:
'Is there anybody out there?'

BBC podcast

Are you nuts for thinking yes or crazy for thinking no? A big conversation to enjoy.

What is your earliest memory?

Grandma

Leaving the pots and pans and a chopping board full of ingredients, my grandmother motioned me aside. I'd thought better of entering her kitchen before a meal as I had a habit of getting in the way. I was 'there to eat' not to 'impede the process' or 'create distraction'.

We left the kitchen and stood by the laundry door. The dirty washing looked on from the basket on top of the machine. I sensed I was about to receive some advice. I leant down to ensure I could hear clearly as she began to speak.

'I hope this teaches you a lesson,' my grandmother said.

I was confused. 'What teaches me? What lesson?'

'Your divorce,' she said bluntly.

'My divorce?'

'Yes, yes. Your divorce. I hope your divorce teaches you a lesson.'

'And what lesson would that be?'

'Never to fall in love again,' she said.

I paused to digest this before offering a question in response. 'If I choose never to love again then what do I have?'

She shook her head gently before walking back into the kitchen.

The conversation was over.

Watch:
Freestyle skate-boardist

Rodney Mullen

Possibly the best 'pro'
I've seen in any sport.
Someone who is their craft.
And yet there is always
room to improve.

Is
perfect
possible?

What is
worth
fighting
for?

View:
Tiananmen's
'Tank Man'

Jeff Widener
photograph

An extraordinary display
of strength and/or courage
from which you can
investigate the question
and beyond.

Rakim

Rakim Allah aka William Michael Griffin Jr. was the first
Muslim I ever met.

Not that I was counting or, for that matter, looking to catalogue
people by their faith. I was just guessing. It was his name, of
course, and what he said, combined with a little background
knowledge on my part. Rakim was a member of the Five
Percent Nation, a religious movement formed in the sixties of
which I knew nothing and still don't as I can't count what I've
read to be gospel. So to of Christianity, Hinduism, Judaism,
Taoism, Buddhism and more. My exposure to each has been
limited by choice. I'd skipped religious education at school
thanks to a pointed note from my parents and a strong sense of

self-belief and purpose. I do remember joining my classmates on a bland school excursion where we were bussed about various religious buildings in our neighbourhood. We visited a Christian church, a Catholic church, then a Protestant church and possibly a Baptist church. We'd leave an unkempt and gruff bus driver behind as we walked in pairs towards each entrance where a priest greeted us in his religious garb. Each church proudly promoted its nuances. It felt like a hard sell from a soft voice. I decided that the buildings were essentially the same – a cookie cutter used to define each man and his voice and the same figure brutally nailed to a cross. Sometimes He would be a simple wooden carving; sometimes a colourful porcelain type recreation complete with weeping wounds that made me feel uneasy. I don't recall much from that day. I was neither engaged nor inspired. I do remember thinking that He was an extraordinary symbol, but for exactly what I wasn't sure. Amplification?

Meeting Rakim Allah was different. His appearance alone was enough to interest me: resplendent in leisure suits, gold chains, and high top 'wheels' that oozed street cred. But it was his words and the way he delivered them that made me want to invest. He had a stately approach which gave him gravitas. He talked persuasively, his voice raw and real. Although we were worlds apart, everything he said cut through. I wanted to hear more. The idea that he was Muslim didn't change a thing. He spat tight rhymes over dope beats and that was enough for me.

I bought cassettes of 'Paid in full' and its successor 'Follow the leader' and put them both on high rotation. I'd torture the plastic cogs for hours, fast forwarding and rewinding as I sifted through every lyric. I'd angle my speakers so as to best rebound the sound around my bedroom and tweak the naff equaliser trying to extract extra bass on songs like 'I ain't no joke', only to distort the sound and ruin the epic intro.

Time spent listening to Rakim Allah led me to Big Daddy Kane, Public Enemy, Jungle Brothers, A Tribe Called Quest and KRS-One, who suggested I 'Step into a world' – which I did. I indulged as much of the 'golden age' of hip hop as I could get my ears around and my hands on. It got me thinking, wanting to learn about others and about myself. Music became my religion. It answered my questions, while asking others. It gave me strength and direction. It still does.

I was as shocked to see the 'Paid in full' film clip late one night featuring Israeli singer Ofra Haza as I was to see two planes fly into New York's Twin Towers many years later. Was I shocked by a Muslim? Or by people showcasing all that is good and bad in this world? I've spent time since thinking about it, and I see the actions of people against the adjunct of religion. I respect the beliefs of others, their want to serve and to pray. To each their own. If I were to display my devotion I think I'd kneel before a record spinning Ganesh and give thanks to Rakim Allah and 'all' who make music. I'd pray for less less abject horror and more stirring film clips. And for the world to promote people ahead of creed.

Watch:
Larry Clark's
'Kids' clip

YouTube videos

A brilliant gut-punch
that shines light into the
raw world of adolescent
behaviour. A conversation
starter.

What is
safe sex?

Watch:
Bladerunner 2049

Denis Villeneuve's film

A memorable movie
that overloads the senses
and provides a creative
launchpad for discussion.

Are computers smarter than people?

Does it matter what you wear?

Read about:
Designer
Hugo Boss

It is said that 'clothes maketh the man', in this case one has to wonder what type of man. The power of fashion and brand is real.

ADVENTURES

EXPLORE
NEW WAYS

ANYWHERE
NO QUESTION

Her façade was grand, an exact blend of designer labels, high-end jewellery, gaudy shoes and thickly caked makeup. Each designed strategically within her mind to work in unison to mask from the casual onlooker, work colleague or mirrored image the fact that she was walkin on a tight rope.

Her gaze would shift quickly back to her crimson shoes each and every time she caught a glimpse of her reflection. Better to look upon pretty things than deal with reality. She had casually started towards the final weeks of her summer holidays just doing the odd bit of blow. It helped smooth the edges of her square peg. She had never found her place, not that she had looked, and a toot of coke allowed her to forget about the search. Life had always been served on a platter. That year was marked 'gap' for self-exploration before she would return to a commerce degree. Years on, the only gap would be that in her life; empty pages that would always remain so. She was never the only one doing it. There were always others – a cast of thousands who found solace in substance. Girlfriends, boyfriends, lovers and the guy who sat next to her now had all been there and done that but didn't share her sense of indulgence. Over time they seemed to move on. Treading water may be the hardest thing to do and yet she made it look easy. Broken promises, hearts, bones and windows marked her territory. With her focus upon her shoes and their intricate leatherwork she thought of a promise. *I will never inject*. The scars between her toes announced that promise broken along with 'only at parties' and 'never for sex'. For her it was more than just the after-effect. It was a lifestyle rush with the lead being as rewarding as the result. Before Coke, Flake, Snow, Angel Dust, C, Toot, Base she felt life was dull. Not everyone's life, just hers. In her mind, life was cornflake bland and everyone else was indulging the sweetest sugary treats. She had little time for her co-worker or his social commentary. She was beyond caring about the direction of government. She was tuned out to his musings but highly aware of her surroundings. She had already scoped each and every person aboard. Maybe a little 'Horse' today if she could find someone to fit the saddle. No joy to be found here. She would have to wait for her regular. Running her tongue about her fraying teeth and religiously wiping her nose it was obvious that time was catching up. Her body told a story, from her collapsing nasal cavities to the small bruises her sleeve. She was falling without a safety net. Her company didn't care beyond his efforts to publicly announce that she was within his personal space and she wasn't aware of anyone who could help her, at least not within this carriage.

His dark skin highlighted by the rich colours of his clothes made his form obvious and yet I'd never taken the time to notice. They were truly loud garments whose design said tribalism.

Sport, like society, is centered on acceptance; your team, my team. He is some distance from the sporting teams of New York whose logos adorn his shirt and yet that is where most would see his origins. Society sees a turbo Negro hell bent on destroying the very fabric of community with his arsenal of weapons. Particularly that drum-based 'rap' music whose lyrics preach hatred and violence. The truth is he has no iPod and his clothing is stitched cheaply in China by a faceless girl and sold at a reasonable rate in the stores by a faceless woman. The manufacturer knows that erroneous 'rip-offs' will be tolerated if the rack price is right. Part profit will be used to redesign the ageing face of the manufacturer's wife. As a ghost in this space his budget is limited. Besides, it's not what you wear but how you wear it and he knew how to wear it; it was all he had. The Horn of Africa is a long way from NY's 42nd Street or for that matter platform 5. All he wanted to do was fit in and go about his business. Fly under the radar. Such a plan was executed in his homeland, quite literally. He had witnessed each of his loved ones die at the end of a sixty-dollar Kalashnikov. Hatred comes cheaply. No family would follow in his footsteps to port and aboard a container ship bound for anywhere other than there. He lived like an animal in order to survive and will continue to do so until he can fabricate a plan beyond his next meal. Those about him now are scared of him, particularly the sense of desperate strength. Trust is a dirty word for all involved. And yet somehow he will find the courage to again believe and as such receive a great gift of friendship from a faintly pinstriped dark suit into which he would bump while trying to avoid eye contact with those about him. The suit would belong to a QC whose knowledge of refugees was born of a deep passion for human rights and an ability to assist in the restructure of dislocated life. Risk versus reward would pay dividends.

Dib-Dib-Dob-Dob. I couldn't remember if that was Boy Scout or Girl Guide gibberish.

———————————————

Regardless, she simply reeked of disciplined home economics although her basic blouse didn't announce her domestic skills via an array of carefully sewn on patches. She could cook. She could clean. She could tie a rope. Nobody issues a badge of honor for suicide. Although she sat among the other eastbound passengers she really wasn't there. She held her purse so tightly the veins in her hand were purple. Offset to her right an unintentionally urban kitsch shopping trolley was filled to the brim with food. She however wasn't interested in trends. Practicality was always the bottom line. Dozens of stone fruits, assorted vegetables and the leanest beef caused the weathered canvas to swell. Multiple casseroles, some bulked with pasta, others rice and stewed fruit medleys. In three more stops she'd alight the train. Hours ahead of her family's meal time, her planning is exact. There is time to prepare everything except their reaction, but in such a mental state the 't' in outcome may be the only 't' that hasn't been crossed. A long favoured Scout motto involves the performance of 'a good turn daily'. In her mind this was hers. She thought herself a burden now. She was a lady of action; always had been. Growing up on a farm there was no time to waste dilly-dallying. The fields must be irrigated, the hay bailed and any animal that was in pain dealt with swiftly; a bullet to the head. Don't get caught up in the emotion of the moment, simply move on. City life meant that she no longer had access to a gun. She had to think outside the square. She would burn her arm lightly later that day while adding an extra cup of pasta to an already hearty broth in an attempt to please her husband and two sons. And her thumbs would sting from snapping tight seventeen Tupperware containers that would just squeeze inside the freezer on the second attempt. Tupperware Tetris. Everything about the house would be cleaned, polished, dusted and arranged within an inch of its life and so hers would expire after deliberately stepping off a vinyl covered kitchen chair in the garage. She would choose the seat to ensure it could be easily cleaned. She was a practical woman. Those she sat among paid her no attention.

Are our lives private?

Listen:
'Is Privacy Dead'

BBC podcast

In the digital age, it's worthwhile thinking about what's personal and what's public.

 Username

 Password

 Remember me Forgot password?

LOGIN

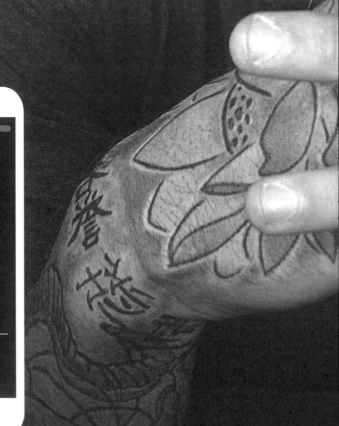

Is there danger in being **an indivdual?**

**Watch:
Fuel Tank
Feature
11 about
Japan's
Skyline
Kaido racer**

A stark example of being
authentic at the expense
of external ridicule.

Who are the world leaders?

Read: Rosa Parks

Civil Rights activist

True leadership has the strength to stand with conviction. And shares a voice that resonates beyond a moment in time.

Acknowledgments

The author and publisher would like to thank Oskar, Archi and Shoshi, Kara Reardon, Jessica Blizzard, Michael Hirsh, Jo Ingles, Jane Kennedy, Tommy Little, Jarryd Roughead, Jo Silvagni, Harvey Silver and Adam Spencer for their support; as well as the following for their generosity in providing images for the book: Riley Muscat (page iii); Agung Wiranatha @goesagoenks and Ade Krisna Dwipayana @adekrisnadwipayana (pages 14-15); Gavin Coath @c04th (page 21 and pages 64-65); Masrur Alam Chowdhury @gunner.masrur (pages 24-25); Jarman Impey @ jarmanimpey (pages 34-35); Jessica Heinrich @jessicaevierose (pages 52-53); Hope Shadbolt @hopeshadbolt (pages 62-63); Sam Morel @Supersonic64 (pages 76-77); Rob Sayers @ kaidospec (pages 84-85); Briar Rose Kershaw @theebriarrose (page 91) and Ali Mozaffari @mozaffary.ali (pages 126-127); Marta Martínez @marta_fresa (pages 106-107); Alicia Harvey @aliciaharvey__ and Chaise Eade @chaiseinator and @chsn8r (pages 108-109); Sasha Nickels (page 113); Tony John (pages 124-125); and Santiago Hurtado @santgazi (page 137). All other images Adobe Stock.